All About
ROSH HASHANAH

by
Judyth Groner
Madeline Wikler

illustrated by
Bonnie Gordon-Lucas

KAR-BEN COPIES, INC.
Rockville, MD

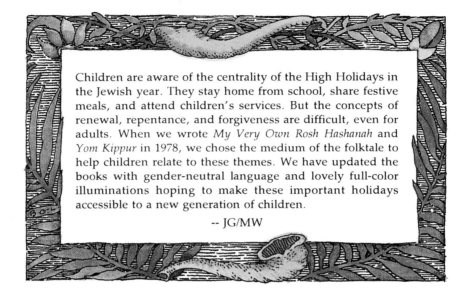

Children are aware of the centrality of the High Holidays in the Jewish year. They stay home from school, share festive meals, and attend children's services. But the concepts of renewal, repentance, and forgiveness are difficult, even for adults. When we wrote *My Very Own Rosh Hashanah* and *Yom Kippur* in 1978, we chose the medium of the folktale to help children relate to these themes. We have updated the books with gender-neutral language and lovely full-color illuminations hoping to make these important holidays accessible to a new generation of children.

-- JG/MW

Library of Congress Cataloging-in-Publication Data

Groner, Judyth Saypol
All About Rosh Hashanah / Judyth Groner and Madeline Wikler:
illustrated by Bonnie Gordon-Lucas.
p.   cm.
Summary: Brief text introduces the history and customs of Rosh
Hashanah, the Jewish New Year. Includes folk tales.
ISBN 1-58013-004-6 (pbk.)
1. Rosh ha-Shanah — Juvenile literature. [1. Rosh ha-Shanah.
2. Fasts and feasts — Judaism.] I. Wikler, Madeline, 1943-
II. Gordon-Lucas, Bonnie, ill. III. Title
BM695.N5G75   1997
296.4'315—dc21   97-2697
                                                                           CIP
                                                                            AC

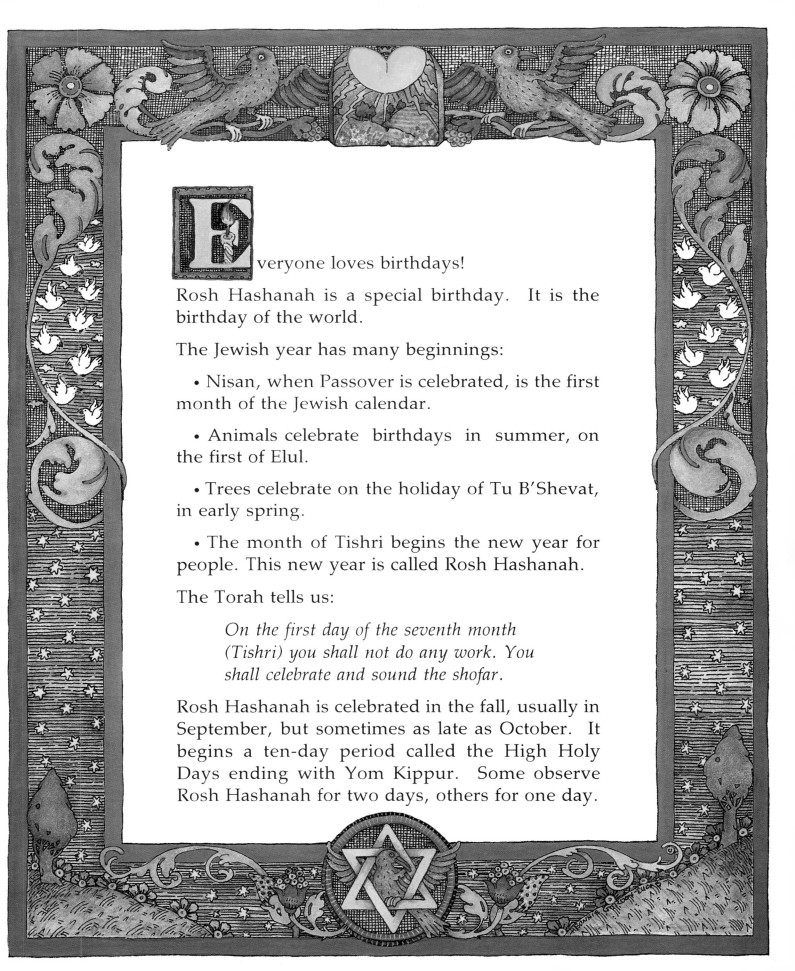

Everyone loves birthdays!

Rosh Hashanah is a special birthday. It is the birthday of the world.

The Jewish year has many beginnings:

• Nisan, when Passover is celebrated, is the first month of the Jewish calendar.

• Animals celebrate birthdays in summer, on the first of Elul.

• Trees celebrate on the holiday of Tu B'Shevat, in early spring.

• The month of Tishri begins the new year for people. This new year is called Rosh Hashanah.

The Torah tells us:

On the first day of the seventh month (Tishri) you shall not do any work. You shall celebrate and sound the shofar.

Rosh Hashanah is celebrated in the fall, usually in September, but sometimes as late as October. It begins a ten-day period called the High Holy Days ending with Yom Kippur. Some observe Rosh Hashanah for two days, others for one day.

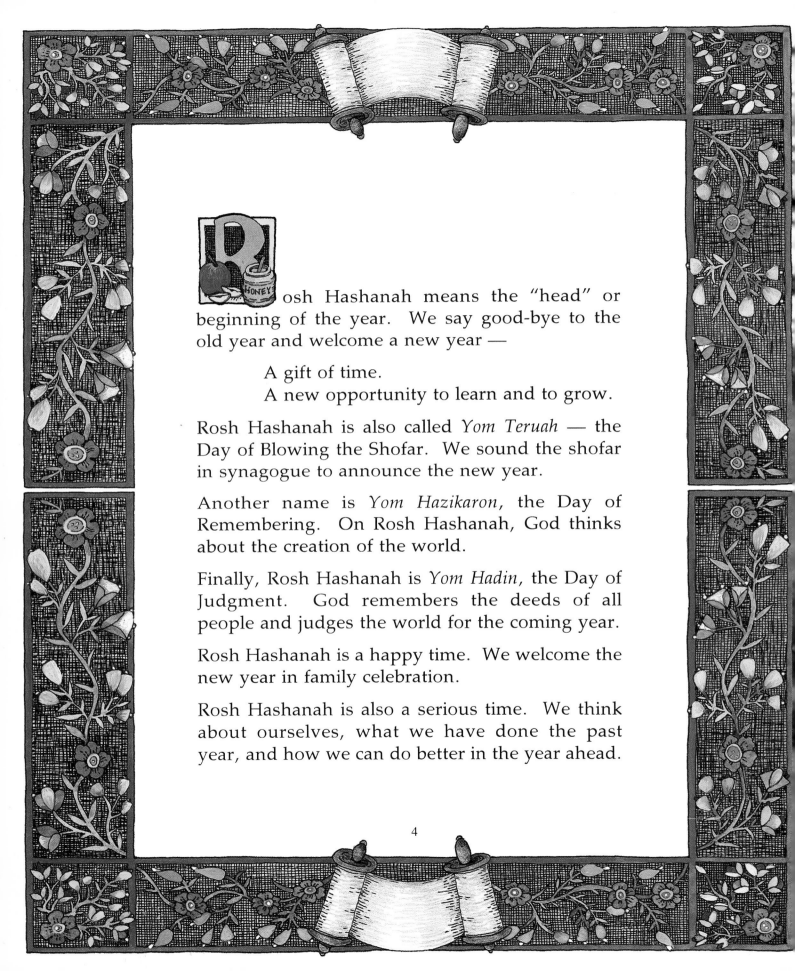

Rosh Hashanah means the "head" or beginning of the year. We say good-bye to the old year and welcome a new year —

> A gift of time.
> A new opportunity to learn and to grow.

Rosh Hashanah is also called *Yom Teruah* — the Day of Blowing the Shofar. We sound the shofar in synagogue to announce the new year.

Another name is *Yom Hazikaron*, the Day of Remembering. On Rosh Hashanah, God thinks about the creation of the world.

Finally, Rosh Hashanah is *Yom Hadin*, the Day of Judgment. God remembers the deeds of all people and judges the world for the coming year.

Rosh Hashanah is a happy time. We welcome the new year in family celebration.

Rosh Hashanah is also a serious time. We think about ourselves, what we have done the past year, and how we can do better in the year ahead.

Once during Elul, the great Rabbi Levi Yitzchak of Berditchev was standing at his window. A shoemaker passed and asked him, "Have you anything to mend?"

Immediately Rabbi Levi Yitzchak began to cry. "Woe is me," he wailed. "Rosh Hashanah, the Day of Judgment, is almost here, and I still have not mended myself."

———————————— ❧ ————————————

A man had lost his way in the forest and wandered for several days. Finally, he saw someone approaching and called out. "Brother! I have been wandering in the forest for several days. Please tell me which is the right way out."

The other responded, "I do not know the way out either, for I have wandered for many days. But I can tell you this. Do not take the way I have gone, for that will lead you astray. Now let us look for the right way together."

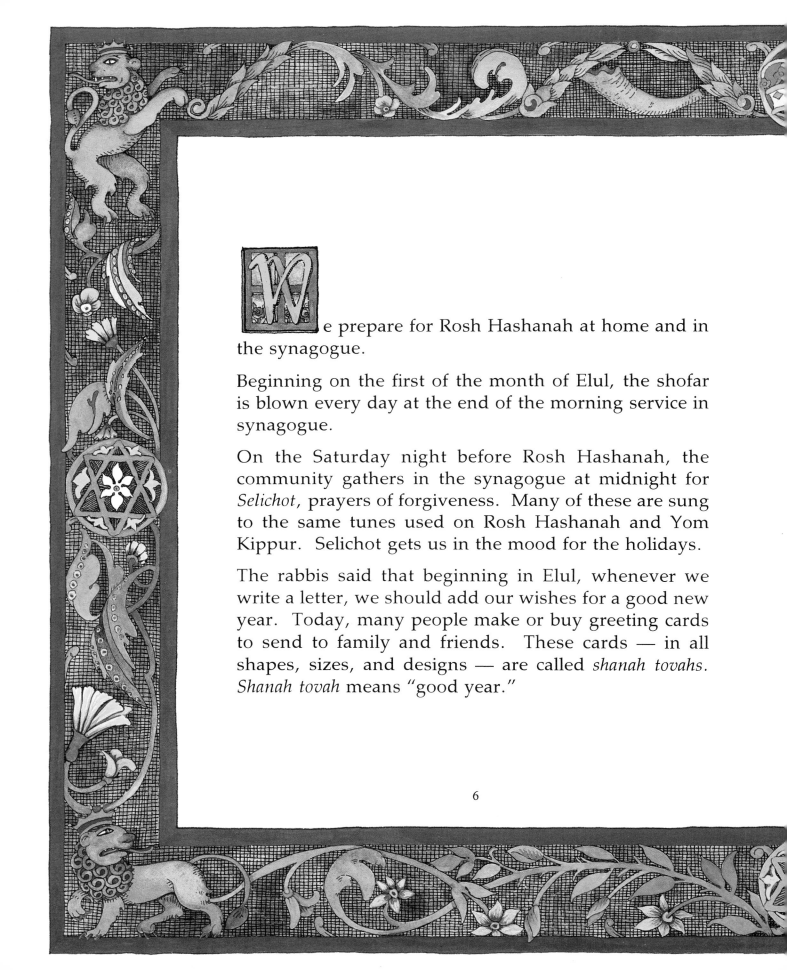

We prepare for Rosh Hashanah at home and in the synagogue.

Beginning on the first of the month of Elul, the shofar is blown every day at the end of the morning service in synagogue.

On the Saturday night before Rosh Hashanah, the community gathers in the synagogue at midnight for *Selichot*, prayers of forgiveness. Many of these are sung to the same tunes used on Rosh Hashanah and Yom Kippur. Selichot gets us in the mood for the holidays.

The rabbis said that beginning in Elul, whenever we write a letter, we should add our wishes for a good new year. Today, many people make or buy greeting cards to send to family and friends. These cards — in all shapes, sizes, and designs — are called *shanah tovahs*. *Shanah tovah* means "good year."

6

n the villages of Eastern Europe where many of our grandparents and great-grandparents once lived, the month before Rosh Hashanah was a busy time.

Cantors and choirs practiced their chants for the special synagogue services. Peddlers went from village to village selling prayer books and prayer shawls. People collected *tzedakah*, contributions for those in need, so everyone would be able to celebrate the holiday.

It was the custom for the *shamash*, the synagogue caretaker, to awaken villagers for early morning prayers. He knocked on their doors with a special hammer carved in the shape of a shofar. Children loved to help. Some would tie strings to their feet and hang the ends out their windows. The shamash would pull the strings to wake the youngsters so they could follow him on his rounds.

very Friday during the month of Elul the Rabbi of Nemirov would vanish. He was nowhere to be seen. Where could the rabbi be?

In heaven, no doubt, the people thought. He's in heaven asking God to bring peace in the New Year.

Where could the rabbi be? A villager decided to find out.

One night he sneaked into the rabbi's home, slid under the rabbi's bed, and waited. Just before dawn, the rabbi awakened, got out of bed, and began to dress. He put on work pants, high boots, a big hat, a coat, and a wide belt. He put a rope in his pocket, tucked an ax in his belt, and left the house. The villager followed.

The rabbi crept in the shadows to woods at the edge of town. He took the ax, chopped down a small tree, and split it into logs. Then he bundled the wood, tied it with the rope, put it on his back, and began walking.

He stopped beside a small, broken-down shack and knocked at the window.

"Who is there?" asked a frightened voice inside.

"It is I, Vassil the peasant," answered the rabbi. "I have wood to sell." He entered the house and found an old woman shivering in the cold.

"I am a poor widow. Where will I get the money?" she asked.

"I'll lend it to you," replied the rabbi.

"How will I pay you back?" asked the woman.

"I will trust you," said the rabbi.

The rabbi put the wood into the oven, kindled the fire, and left without a word.

Now whenever anyone reports that the rabbi has gone to heaven, the villager adds softly, "Heaven? If not higher."

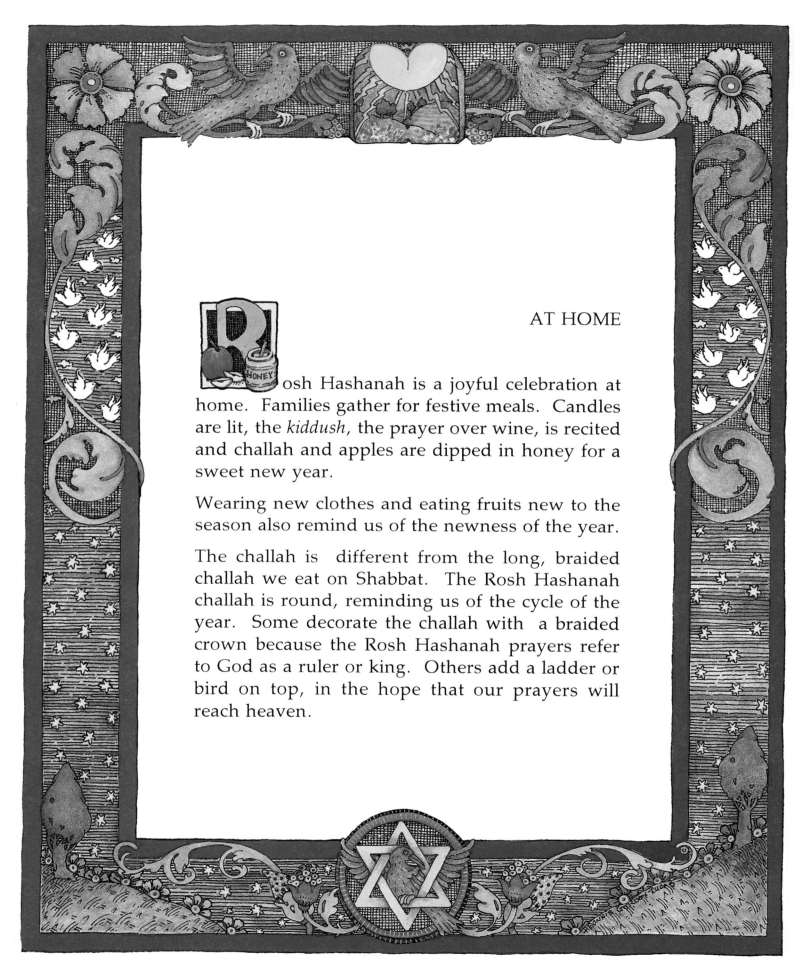

AT HOME

Rosh Hashanah is a joyful celebration at home. Families gather for festive meals. Candles are lit, the *kiddush*, the prayer over wine, is recited and challah and apples are dipped in honey for a sweet new year.

Wearing new clothes and eating fruits new to the season also remind us of the newness of the year.

The challah is different from the long, braided challah we eat on Shabbat. The Rosh Hashanah challah is round, reminding us of the cycle of the year. Some decorate the challah with a braided crown because the Rosh Hashanah prayers refer to God as a ruler or king. Others add a ladder or bird on top, in the hope that our prayers will reach heaven.

There was once a man who was quite forgetful. When he got up in the morning, he never remembered where he left his clothes.

One night he thought of a plan. He took paper and pencil, and as he undressed, he wrote down exactly where he put all his clothes.

The next morning he was very pleased. He took the piece of paper and read the list.

"Cap." There it was. "Pants." He found them. "Shirt." There it lay. And so it was until he was fully dressed.

"That's fine," he said. "But now, where am I myself?" he asked very puzzled. "Where in the world am I?"

He looked and looked, but could not find himself.

Rosh Hashanah gives us a chance to find ourselves.

IN THE SYNAGOGUE

At Rosh Hashanah services the rabbi and cantor wear white robes called *kittels*. The Torah scrolls, too, are dressed in white covers. White stands for forgiveness.

The Rosh Hashanah prayerbook, called the *machzor*, has special prayers of thanks for all the good things God has done for us in the past year. In other prayers we ask God for a happy and peaceful year for ourselves, our families, and all people.

When the synagogue service is over, we greet each other saying, *L'shanah Tovah Tikatevu*, May you be written in the Book of Life for a good year.

———————————— ᔥ ————————————

One of the most important prayers describes God judging the world and writing the judgment in the Book of Life.

It is Rosh Hashanah.
God sits on a throne
And opens a book
Containing a list of all the things
We have done the past year.
The great Shofar is sounded.
As sheep are counted by the shepherd,
One by one
Each of our lives comes before God.
God judges us for the coming year
And writes our judgment in the Book of Life:

Who shall live and who shall die.
Who shall be rich and who shall be poor.
Who shall be at peace and who shall worry.
Who shall rest and who shall wander.

The Book is kept open for ten days.
We have the power
To change the judgment
Through prayer, forgiveness, and good deeds.
At the end of Yom Kippur
The Book is closed.

*O*n Rosh Hashanah when it was time to blow the shofar, the Great Rabbi Levi Yitzchak of Berditchev stood silent on the bimah. The people waited and waited, and nothing happened. They waited some more and still the rabbi did not begin.

Finally the cantor approached the rabbi and asked him what was causing the delay. The rabbi whispered, "A young child just came into the synagogue. He is seated near the door. I overheard him talking. This is what he said:

> *God of the World:*
> *I do not know how to pray.*
> *I do not know what to say.*
> *I only know the letters of the alphabet.*
> *Let me say them to You:*
> *Alef, Bet, Gimel, Dalet...*
> *I give You these letters.*
> *Please join them together*
> *And make up a prayer that will be pleasing to You.*

"The child recited the alphabet to the very end," said Rabbi Levi Yitzchak. "God is busy composing a prayer. We must wait until God is finished. Then we will blow the shofar."

God accepts all prayers that come from the heart.

BLOWING THE SHOFAR

The *shofar* is a musical instrument made from the curved horn of a ram or goat. It is hard to blow and takes a lot of practice.

In ancient Israel, the shofar was used to announce the new moon and holidays, to signal armies, and to call people to attention.

We blow the shofar on Rosh Hashanah —

- to announce the beginning of the year.
- to remind us that God is our ruler and judge.
- to warn us that we need to improve.

The blowing of the shofar is very dramatic. Leaders of the congregation take the Torah scrolls from the Holy Ark and stand beside the shofar blower who recites the blessing commanding us to hear the shofar. As the name of each note is announced, the sound is made:

Tekiyah…Shevarim…Teruah…Tekiyah Gedolah

The final blast, *Tekiyah Gedolah*, is very, very long. Everyone waits anxiously to see how long the shofar blower can hold the note.

*O*nce it happened that a boy from a small village came to the city for the first time.

In the middle of the night he was awakened by the loud beating of drums. He asked the innkeeper what the noise meant. He was told that when a fire breaks out, the people beat their drums, and before long the fire is gone.

When the boy returned home, he told the village leaders about this wonderful system for putting out fires. The people were excited and ordered drums for every household.

The next time a fire broke out, the people beat their drums. As they waited for the fire to go out, many homes burned to the ground.

A visitor asked what was happening. When told of the fire and the drums, he exclaimed, "Do you think you can put out a fire by beating drums? Drums only sound an alarm so the people will wake up and go to the well for water to put out the fire."

Blowing the shofar is also an alarm, warning us to change our ways.

TASHLICH

ashlich means to "toss away." The tashlich ceremony is an imaginary way of "tossing away" our bad deeds.

On the afternoon of Rosh Hashanah families gather on the banks of a river, stream, or pond and recite prayers asking for forgiveness. Then they shake out the dust from their pockets, or they throw breadcrumbs into the water, as if they were getting rid of their bad deeds.

————————————ꙮ————————————

Rosh Hashanah is only a beginning.

For the next ten days, we think about the year that has passed and the year that is to come. These days are called the Days of Forgiveness. On the tenth day we celebrate Yom Kippur, the Day of Atonement.

Home Service for
ROSH HASHANAH

TZEDAKAH

In the villages of Eastern Europe where many of our grandparents and great-grandparents were born, it was a custom before the New Year for a messenger to go from house to house with a sack. Those who could afford it put coins into the sack. Those who were poor took coins from the sack. No one knew who gave and who took. No one was embarrassed to be poor. Every family had money to buy the things needed to celebrate the holiday.

Giving *tzedakah*, sharing what we have with those in need, is an important *mitzvah*, commandment, in Jewish life.

Before Rosh Hashanah begins, we remember this mitzvah by setting aside some of our allowance or savings to help others.

HADLAKAT NEROT
CANDLE-LIGHTING

We welcome Rosh Hashanah by lighting the candles.

בָּרוּךְ אַתָּה יְיָ אֱלֹהֵינוּ מֶלֶךְ הָעוֹלָם,
אֲשֶׁר קִדְּשָׁנוּ בְּמִצְוֹתָיו וְצִוָּנוּ
לְהַדְלִיק נֵר שֶׁל (שַׁבָּת וְשֶׁל) יוֹם טוֹב.

Baruch Atah Adonai Eloheinu Melech ha'olam,
Asher kid'shanu b'mitzvotav v'tzivanu
L'hadlik ner shel (Shabbat v'shel) Yom Tov.

בָּרוּךְ אַתָּה יְיָ אֱלֹהֵינוּ מֶלֶךְ הָעוֹלָם,
שֶׁהֶחֱיָנוּ וְקִיְּמָנוּ וְהִגִּיעָנוּ לַזְּמַן הַזֶּה.

Baruch Atah Adonai Eloheinu Melech ha'olam,
Shehecheyanu, vekiy'manu v'higiyanu laz'man hazeh.

Thank you, God, for bringing us together
to celebrate Rosh Hashanah,
and for the mitzvah of lighting the candles.

May God bless us with a year of joy.
May God bless us with a year of health.
May God bless us with a year of peace.

KIDDUSH
BLESSING OVER WINE

The Kiddush proclaims the holiness of Rosh Hashanah. We sing blessings over the cup of wine in honor of the new year.

בָּרוּךְ אַתָּה יְיָ אֱלֹהֵינוּ מֶלֶךְ הָעוֹלָם,
בּוֹרֵא פְּרִי הַגָּפֶן.

Baruch Atah Adonai Eloheinu Melech ha'olam,
Borei p'ri hagafen.

בָּרוּךְ אַתָּה יְיָ אֱלֹהֵינוּ מֶלֶךְ הָעוֹלָם,
שֶׁהֶחֱיָנוּ וְקִיְּמָנוּ וְהִגִּיעָנוּ לַזְּמַן הַזֶּה.

Baruch Atah Adonai Eloheinu Melech ha'olam,
Shehecheyanu, vekiy'manu v'higiyanu laz'man hazeh.

Thank You, God, for the grapes that grow
from which wine is made for our new year celebration.

Thank You, God, for bringing our friends and family
together to celebrate the new year.

HAMOTZI
CHALLAH BLESSING

The challah we eat on Rosh Hashanah is different from the long, braided challah we eat on Shabbat. It is round, reminding us of the cycle of the year. As we share the challah, we are grateful for the earth and its harvest.

בָּרוּךְ אַתָּה יְיָ אֱלֹהֵינוּ מֶלֶךְ הָעוֹלָם,
הַמּוֹצִיא לֶחֶם מִן הָאָרֶץ.

Baruch Atah Adonai Eloheinu Melech ha'olam,
Hamotzi lechem min ha'aretz.

Thank You, God,
for the blessing of bread,
and for the festive meal
which we will now enjoy together.

BLESSING FOR
A SWEET NEW YEAR

Before we eat, we share apples dipped in honey.

בָּרוּךְ אַתָּה יְיָ אֱלֹהֵינוּ מֶלֶךְ הָעוֹלָם,
בּוֹרֵא פְּרִי הָעֵץ.

Baruch Atah Adonai Eloheinu Melech ha'olam,
Borei p'ri ha'etz.

יְהִי רָצוֹן מִלְפָנֶיךָ יְיָ אֱלֹהֵינוּ
וֵאלֹהֵי אֲבוֹתֵינוּ וְאִמוֹתֵינוּ
שֶׁתְּחַדֵשׁ עָלֵינוּ שָׁנָה טוֹבָה וּמְתוּקָה.

Yehi ratzon milfanecha Adonai Eloheinu
V'elohei avoteinu v'imoteinu
Shet'chadesh aleinu shanah tovah u'metukah.

God of our ancestors,
as we eat this fruit of the trees,
we pray that the new year
will be sweet and happy for all of us.

BIRKAT HAMAZON
AFTER THE MEAL

We join in giving thanks for the festive meal.

בָּרוּךְ אַתָּה יְיָ, הַזָּן אֶת־הַכֹּל.

Baruch Atah Adonai, hazan et hakol.

עֹשֶׂה שָׁלוֹם בִּמְרוֹמָיו הוּא יַעֲשֶׂה שָׁלוֹם
עָלֵינוּ וְעַל כָּל־יִשְׂרָאֵל. וְאִמְרוּ אָמֵן.

Oseh shalom bimromav hu ya'aseh shalom
Aleinu v'al kol Yisrael. Ve'imru amen.

Thank you, God,
for the festive meal we have shared,
for the food we have eaten at this table,
for the Torah and mitzvot which guide our lives,
for Israel, the homeland of the Jewish people,
for our freedom to live as Jews,
for life, strength, and health.
Bless our family, and grant us a good year.

LIGHTING THE CANDLES

Freely adapted after a version
by A.W. BINDER

Freely, as a chant

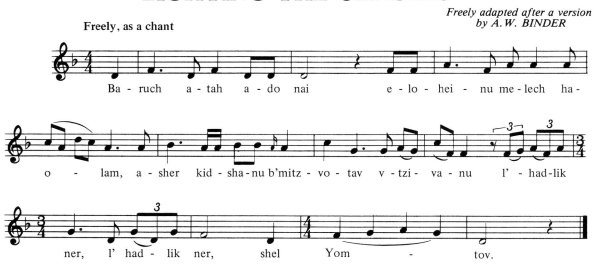

Ba - ruch a - tah a - do nai e - lo - hei - nu me - lech ha - o - lam, a - sher kid - sha - nu b'mitz - vo - tav v'tzi - va - nu l' - had - lik ner, l' - had - lik ner, shel Yom - tov.

SHEHECHEYANU

Traditional

Ba - ruch a - tah a - do nai e - lo - hei - nu me - lech ha - o - lam she - he - che - ya - nu v' - kiy' - ma - nu v' - hi - gi - ya - nu la - z'man ha - zeh.

L'SHANAH TOVAH

Traditional

L' - sha - nah to - vah ti - ka - te - vu, l' - sha - nah to - vah ti - ka - te - vu, ti - ka - te - vu v' - te - cha - te - mu.

26

KIDDUSH

Traditional

SHANAH TOVAH

Sha - nah chal - fah sha - nah av -
rah va - a - ni ya - dai a - ri - ma ____
____ sha - nah to - vah le - cha a -
ba sha - nah to - vah lach ___ i -
ma sha - nah to - vah sha - nah to - vah.

TEKIYAH

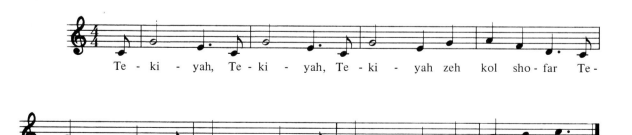

Te - ki - yah, Te - ki - yah, Te - ki - yah zeh kol sho - far Te -
ki - yah, Te - ki - yah, Te - ki - yah sha - nah to - vah.

TAPUCHIM UD'VASH

Apples and Honey

Folk

1. Ta - pu - chim u - d'vash_____ le - Rosh__ Ha - sha - nah
2. Ap - ples and hon - ey for Rosh__ Ha - sha - nah

Ta - pu - chim u - d'vash_____ le - Rosh__ Ha - sha - nah   Sha -
Ap - ples and hon - ey for Rosh__ Ha - sha - nah   A

nah   to - vah,   sha - nah   me - tu - kah!
good   new__ year,   A   sweet   new__ year!

Ta - pu - chim u - d'vash_____ le - Rosh__ Ha - sha - nah.
Ap - ples and hon - ey for Rosh__ Ha - sha - nah.

BEROSH HASHANAH

Traditional

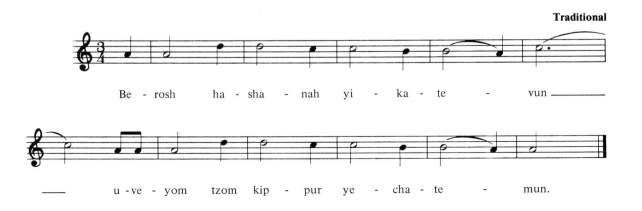

Be - rosh   ha - sha - nah yi - ka - te - vun_____

_____ u - ve - yom tzom kip - pur ye - cha - te - mun.

BIRKAT HAMAZON

M. NATHANSON

OSEH SHALOM

By N. HIRSH

O - seh sha-lom bim-ro-mav hu ya'-a-seh sha-lom a - lei - nu
v' - al kol_ yis-ra - el v'-im-ru, im-ru a -men. O - ru a -men
Ya - a-seh sha-lom Ya - a-seh sha-lom sha - lom a -lei - nu v' - al kol yis-ra-el
Ya - a-seh sha-lom Ya - a-seh sha-lom sha - lom a -lei - nu v' al kol yis-ra - el
ya - a -seh sha-lom ya - a-seh sha-lom sha - lom a -lei - nu v' - al kol yis-ra-el
ya - a-seh sha-lom ya - a-seh sha-lom sha - lom a -lei - nu v' - al kol yis - ra-el
ya - a-seh sha-lom ya - a-seh sha-lom sha - lom a -lei - nu v' - al kol yis - ra- el.